Let's LEARN the BIBLE

Trisha White Priebe

Let's LEARN the BIBLE

A Kids' Guide to God's Word

BARBOUR kidz
A Division of Barbour Publishing

ISBN 979-8-89151-243-6

Published by Barbour Publishing, Inc., 1810 Barbour Drive, Uhrichsville, Ohio 44683, www.barbourbooks.com

Our mission is to inspire the world with the life-changing message of the Bible.

Member of the Evangelical Christian Publishers Association

Printed in China.
002707 1025 XY

For the kids at Central,
This book is for you—with the hope
that you will learn to love God's Word
with your whole heart for your whole
life. There is truly nothing better.
You are loved and prayed for every day.

TABLE OF CONTENTS

Section Four

Section Five

Section Six

Appendix

LET'S LEARN THE BIBLE!

You've made an amazing choice—one that could change your life forever! By opening this book, you're taking a big step toward **learning more about God**. You'll do that by understanding His Word. . .and discovering His incredible plan for your life. In the book you're reading right now, you'll uncover the secrets of **the most powerful Book in the world**—the Bible.

The Bible isn't just a collection of old stories to read on a rainy day. The Bible is alive, it's active, and it's filled with hope and truth. It's your guide when life gets confusing, your comfort when you feel sad. It's like a telescope for seeing God, and a mirror for seeing yourself.

No other book can be what the Bible is, or do what it does. That's because it is actually the Word of God.

Sometimes, the Bible can feel big and overwhelming. That's okay—lots of people have thought that. But the book you hold in your hands is like a map, ready to help you find the Bible's greatest treasures. You'll meet heroes of the faith, find exciting promises, and learn lessons that will help you every single day.

Are you ready to explore the most amazing Book on the planet? ***Let's learn the Bible!***

Section One

WHAT IS THE BIBLE?

WHAT MAKES THE BIBLE SO SPECIAL?

The Bible is the Word of God. That means it's a special message directly from God to you. It's not like other books, because God Himself created it. He "inspired" people to write exactly what He wanted you to know. "Inspired" means God "breathed out" what He wanted them to say. Then the writers put God's thoughts into their own words.

Did you know **the Bible is actually a library of books**? It's not just one big book—it's **a collection of 66 smaller books**. They were written by many men over a very long time. . .more than a thousand years.

The Bible tells us who God is, how much He loves us, and how we can have a relationship with Him. It's filled with amazing stories, important lessons, and promises we can trust.

Everything that was written in the Holy Writings long ago was written to teach us. By not giving up, God's Word gives us strength and hope.

ROMANS 15:4

Have you ever used a flashlight in the dark? **The Bible is like a flashlight**—showing us what's right and helping us make good choices. When we read and follow God's Word, it lights our way and helps us stay on the right path.

Your Word is a lamp to my feet
and a light to my path.
PSALM 119:105

The opening up of Your Word gives light.
It gives understanding to the child-like.
PSALM 119:130

For the word is a lamp. The teaching is a light,
and strong words that punish are the way of life.
PROVERBS 6:23

All this helps us know that what the early preachers said was true. You will do well to listen to what they have said. Their words are as lights that shine in a dark place. Listen until you understand what they have said. Then it will be like the morning light which takes away the darkness. And the Morning Star (Christ) will rise to shine in your hearts.
2 PETER 1:19

HOW CAN THE BIBLE HELP ME?

The Bible is packed with wisdom. It teaches us all about life and shows us exactly how to live. **The Bible helps us understand what's right,** what's wrong, and how to please God. The Bible is much more than any other book—it's a guide for life.

The Bible can help you:

Grow closer to God. As you read, you discover who God really is. You'll learn about His love, kindness, and power. You find out what He's like and how much He cares for you.

Love and care for others. As you study, you learn how to reflect God's love to the world. He'll show you how to be kind, forgive, and be patient with others.

Make wise choices. The Bible is full of stories and teachings that show you how to make better decisions. Wise choices honor God and lead to a better life for you.

Respond to your feelings. The Bible teaches us how to handle our emotions—like anger, sadness, or worry. As always, the Bible helps us to honor God and become better people ourselves.

God created people to have emotions. **The Bible shows us that God cares about our feelings.** We can take all of our feelings to God, trusting Him to guide us through them. He wants to give us peace, no matter what we're going through.

But You, O Lord, are a God full of love and pity. You are slow to anger and rich in loving-kindness and truth.
PSALM 86:15

Big Idea

No matter what you're feeling today, there's a Bible verse to help!

GOD'S WORD FOR BIG FEELINGS

When You're Angry

A gentle answer turns away anger,
but a sharp word causes anger.
PROVERBS 15:1

When You're Sad

The Lord is near to those who have a broken heart.
And He saves those who are broken in spirit.
PSALM 34:18

When You're Scared

Do not fear, for I am with you.
Do not be afraid, for I am your God.
I will give you strength, and for sure
I will help you. Yes, I will hold you up
with My right hand that is right and good.
ISAIAH 41:10

When You're Happy

It is good to give thanks to the Lord,
and sing praises to Your name, O Most High.
It is good to tell of Your loving-kindness
in the morning, and of how faithful You are at night.
PSALM 92:1–2

WHY SHOULD I READ THE BIBLE?

Have you ever felt like reading the Bible is work? Maybe it seems to be a chore, like cleaning your room or putting the dishes away. (If you've ever thought about Bible reading this way, you're not alone!)

But it doesn't have to be that way. Our attitude can change everything. If we think of Bible reading as boring—if it's just something we "have to do"—we will miss out on how amazing it really is. But if we remember that **the Bible is God's Word to us**—filled with His love and wisdom—it will change our lives.

The truth is, **reading the Bible isn't a chore at all.** It's not something we *have* to do, it's something we *get* to do. We read the Bible for two main reasons: to know God better and to learn how to please Him.

Rhyme It!

Always do the things you should.
God is pleased when you do good.

Want to know God better? Here are some verses to help you grow closer to Him:

"You will look for Me and find Me,
when you look for Me with all your heart."
JEREMIAH 29:13

Look for the Lord and His strength.
Look for His face all the time.
PSALM 105:4

Look for the Lord while He may be found.
Call upon Him while He is near.
ISAIAH 55:6

God has shown His love to us by sending His only Son into the world. God did this so we might have life through Christ. This is love! It is not that we loved God but that He loved us. For God sent His Son to pay for our sins with His own blood.
1 JOHN 4:9–10

Want to learn how to please God? Here are some verses to help guide your choices:

O man, He has told you what is good. What does the Lord ask of you but to do what is fair and to love kindness, and to walk without pride with your God?
MICAH 6:8

You must be kind to each other. Think of the other person. Forgive other people just as God forgave you because of Christ's death on the cross.
EPHESIANS 4:32

Religion that is pure and good before God the Father is to help children who have no parents and to care for women whose husbands have died who have troubles. Pure religion is also to keep yourself clean from the sinful things of the world.
JAMES 1:27

HOW DOES GOD SPEAK TO ME?

Getting a letter in the mail is fun. There's something special about a personal message that's just for you. That makes you feel important and loved, doesn't it? Well, **the Bible is like a letter from God**—a message written just for you!

Some people wonder how God speaks to human beings. One of the most important ways is through His Word—the Bible. The Bible is full of God's truth, His wisdom, and His love. When you read it, you hear from God Himself.

Each time you read, **think of the Bible as God's personal note to you.** He's inviting you to know Him better and follow His ways. This is not just any book—it's a letter from the God who created you and wants to be with you.

What could be better than that?

Rhyme It!

God is love! He'll even sing
when you take Him as your king.

If you are a child of God, He has a lot to say to you in His Word. Here are a few verses to get you started. Try to find each one in your Bible and take a moment to read God's own words to you:

God has a good plan for your life.
Read Jeremiah 29:11

Trusting God will help you make wise choices, and He will guide you along the right path in life.
Read Proverbs 3:5–6

God will always be with you, no matter where you go.
Read Matthew 28:20

God is working everything out for your good, even when things don't seem perfect.
Read Romans 8:28

God cares about what's on your mind and heart—so don't be afraid to share things with Him.
Read 1 Peter 5:7

Wow! Think about it—the God who created the whole universe wants to speak directly to *you*. He made the stars, the oceans, and everything else, and He thinks *you* are very, very important. God has special things He wants *you* to know and understand.

ACTIVITY:
How Well Do You Know God's Word?

Are you ready to test your Bible knowledge? This quiz will challenge what you've learned so far and help you discover even more about God's Word! Each question has three possible answers—choose the one you think is correct. Don't worry if you don't know all the answers. . .this is a great way to learn.

1. What is the Bible?

   a) a collection of poems
   b) a special letter from God to you
   c) a book of science facts

2. How many books are in the Bible?

   a) 39
   b) 66
   c) 100

3. What is one way the Bible can help you?

   a) it helps you understand how to cook
   b) it shows you how to make money
   c) it helps you grow closer to God

4. When you're feeling angry, what does the Bible say?

    a) a gentle answer turns away anger
    b) shout at everyone
    c) ignore your feelings

5. What does the Bible say about God's plan for your life?

    a) it's a secret, so don't try to figure it out
    b) you have to make your own plan
    c) God has a good plan for your life

Okay, the quiz is complete. Whether or not you got all the answers right, you're doing a good thing by digging into God's Word. Turn the page to check your answers and see how much you've discovered!

Answers

1 = b
2 = b
3 = c
4 = a
5 = c

Scoring

4–5 correct: You're a Bible expert! Keep reading and learning to know God better every day.

3 correct: Great job! You're on your way to knowing God's Word even better.

1–2 correct: Nice work! There's more to discover. . .keep reading your Bible.

0 correct: No worries! God's Word is full of treasure—keep reading and you'll learn more.

Section Two

WHERE DID THE BIBLE COME FROM?

HOW GOD GAVE US HIS WORD

The Bible was written by many different people over hundreds of years. They lived in different places and had all kinds of different jobs. Some were shepherds, others were kings. Some were fishermen, and one was a doctor! But they all had one thing in common: **God gave the Bible authors a message to write.**

All the Holy Writings are God-given and are made alive by Him.
2 TIMOTHY 3:16

No part of the Holy Writings came long ago because of what man wanted to write. But holy men who belonged to God spoke what the Holy Spirit told them.
2 PETER 1:21

The Bible tells us that **all of scripture was "breathed out" by God.** He gave every writer the ideas to write down. Then God made sure everything they wrote was true and exactly what He wanted us to know. The writers used their own words and styles, but God guided them the whole time.

Here is something amazing: Though the Bible was written over a long, long time, it all fits together perfectly! God was in charge, making sure **His message is clear and correct.**

One way we know that God inspired the words of scripture is a certain phrase you see often in the Bible: "This is what the Lord says."

When you see phrases like that, you can be extra sure the words that follow come straight from God. Hundreds of times in the Bible, men like Isaiah, Jeremiah, and Ezekiel wrote, **"This is what the Lord says."** You can be sure they were writing messages God gave them.

God's Word is living and powerful. It is sharper than a sword that cuts both ways. It cuts straight into where the soul and spirit meet and it divides them. It cuts into the joints and bones. It tells what the heart is thinking about and what it wants to do.

HEBREWS 4:12

Here are some examples when God spoke directly:

This is what the Lord Who made the heavens, the God Who planned and made the earth, and everything in it and did not make it a waste place, but made it a place for people to live in, says, "I am the Lord, and there is no other."
ISAIAH 45:18

The Lord says, "Cursed is the man who trusts in man, who trusts in the flesh for his strength, and whose heart turns away from the Lord."
JEREMIAH 17:5

"For I know the plans I have for you," says the Lord, "plans for well-being and not for trouble, to give you a future and a hope."
JEREMIAH 29:11

Verses like these show us how God speaks to His people to teach, guide, and encourage. Can you find other verses like these in your Bible? Write them down, underline, or highlight them when you discover them.

WHO WROTE THE BIBLE?

God used more than forty different authors to write the words in your Bible. That means He had a whole team of people to share His incredible story with you. Why did God do that? So you could know Him better and learn to live for Him. Isn't that amazing? Now, let's get to know some of those authors and discover how God used them to write His Word!

Moses

Moses is one of the most famous Bible authors. He wrote the first five books of the Bible, telling us about creation, the beginning of God's people, and God's laws. Moses is known for leading the Israelites out of slavery in Egypt and through the wilderness. God spoke to him in special ways, and Moses wrote down what God told him.

The Lord spoke to Moses face to face,
as a man speaks to his friend.
EXODUS 33:11

David

David was a king, a warrior, and a songwriter. He wrote many of the Psalms, which are songs and prayers to God. David's heart was full of love for God, and he poured out his feelings—joy, sadness, fear—through his songs. Some of David's Psalms are still used in worship today.

David the son of Jesse, the man who was raised on high, the chosen one of the God of Jacob, the sweet song writer of Israel. . .
2 SAMUEL 23:1

Isaiah

Isaiah was a prophet who lived in ancient Israel. He wrote the book of Isaiah, which contains God's messages of warning, hope, and promises. Isaiah spoke to kings and the regular people of Israel. He told them about God's plans and a coming Savior—Jesus! Isaiah is known for prophecies—truthful messages about the future—of "the Messiah," Jesus.

At that time the Lord spoke through Isaiah the son of Amoz, saying. . .
ISAIAH 20:2

Paul

Paul was a Christian leader who wrote many letters, also called *epistles*. Paul wrote to churches and to individual people. Some of his letters—to the Romans, Ephesians, and Philippians—are now books in the New Testament. Paul wrote about how to live for God, how to love other people, and how Jesus changed everything for the better.

You can be sure the long waiting of our Lord is part of His plan to save men from the punishment of sin. God gave our dear brother Paul the wisdom to write about this also.
2 PETER 3:15

John

John was one of Jesus' twelve disciples, or chosen followers. He wrote the Gospel of John, as well as three letters—1 John, 2 John, and 3 John—and the book of Revelation. John's writings help us understand how much God loves us and how we should love each other. John also wrote about the end times and the amazing things to come when Jesus returns!

John tells that the Word of God is true. He tells of Jesus Christ and all that he saw and heard of Him. The man who reads this Book and listens to it being read and obeys what it says will be happy.
REVELATION 1:2–3

HOW DID THE BIBLE COME TOGETHER?

The Bible was written over more than one thousand, five hundred years by about forty different authors. Isn't it amazing how God used so many people and so much time to give us His Word?

Let's take a journey through time to see how the Bible was written:

The Books of Moses

(written about 1,400 years before Jesus was born)

Moses wrote the first five books of the Bible, telling us about the beginning of the world, the first people, and God's laws for His people.

Moses wrote the words of this Law in a book from beginning to the end.
DEUTERONOMY 31:24

The Prophets

(written about 1,000 to 400 years before Jesus was born)

God used special people called *prophets* like Isaiah and Jeremiah to write books that taught God's plan and how people should live for Him.

Mercies and forgivenesses belong to the Lord our God, though we have rebelled against Him. Nor have we obeyed the voice of the LORD our God to walk in His laws, which He set before us by His servants the prophets.
DANIEL 9:9–10 SKJV

The Gospels

(written about 40 to 90 after Jesus was born)

Matthew, Mark, Luke, and John wrote about Jesus' life in books called "Gospels"—meaning "good news." They told stories about Jesus' teaching and miracles. They also described His death and how He came back to life.

Many people have written about the things that have happened among us. Those who saw everything from the first and helped teach the Good News have passed these things on to us. Dear Theophilus, I have looked with care into these things from the beginning. I have decided it would be good to write them to you.

LUKE 1:1–3

Letters to the Early Church

(written about 50 to 70 years after Jesus was born)

Paul and other wise leaders wrote letters to the early Christians. These letters help us know how to live for God and love others.

When this letter has been read to you, have it read in the church in Laodicea also. Be sure you read the letter that is coming from Laodicea.

COLOSSIANS 4:16

Revelation

(written about 90 to 100 years after Jesus was born)

John wrote the last book of the Bible called *Revelation*. It tells us what will happen when Jesus comes to earth a second time.

The things that are written in the Book are made known by Jesus Christ. God gave these things to Christ so He could show them to the servants He owns. These are things which must happen very soon. Christ sent His angel to John who is a servant owned by Him. Christ made these things known to John.

REVELATION 1:1

Today

The Bible didn't just appear out of nowhere. Over hundreds and hundreds of years, God "inspired" real people to write His message. He "breathed out" the words and ideas that He wanted the Bible authors to write. Many of these authors were just like you and me—but God used them to share His love, His wisdom, and His plans for the whole world.

The best part? **You get to read God's Word today!** Every story, every lesson, and every promise is there because God wants *you* to know Him better and live for Him.

I will be glad in Your Law, which I love.
I will lift up my hands to Your Word, which I love, and I will think about Your Law.

PSALM 119:47–48

HOW WAS THE BIBLE MADE?

In the beginning, the Bible wasn't a book like you hold in your hands right now. **The Bible was originally written on scrolls**—those are long sheets of writing material made from animal skins or a plant called papyrus. These scrolls were rolled up and stored carefully.

When the Bible was being written, there were no printers or copy machines to help. People called "scribes," who were trained to write things down, copied the words by hand. They double-checked their work, over and over again, to make sure the message stayed the same.

Scribes spent long hours making sure they didn't make mistakes. One wrong letter could change the meaning of God's Word, and they didn't want that. **The Bible is too important to handle it carelessly.**

Try Being a Scribe

Practice copying God's Word, just like the ancient scribes did. See how well you can do!

Pick one of the following verses to copy. (Or if you want, choose your own favorite verse from your own copy of the Bible.) Write the verse on a piece of paper or in a notebook. Try to copy it as perfectly as you can, just like the scribes did.

Your Word is a lamp to my feet
and a light to my path.
PSALM 119:105

"For I know the plans I have for you," says the Lord, "plans for well-being and not for trouble, to give you a future and a hope."
JEREMIAH 29:11

"For God so loved the world that He gave His only Son. Whoever puts his trust in God's Son will not be lost but will have life that lasts forever."
JOHN 3:16

I can do all things because Christ gives me the strength.
PHILIPPIANS 4:13

We love Him because He loved us first.
1 JOHN 4:19

If you want, share your copied verse with someone—maybe a friend, a parent, or your pastor! Tell them why you picked that verse and what it means to you.

DO YOU KNOW THESE AMAZING BIBLE FACTS?

By now you know the Bible is no ordinary book. But did you know the Bible also has an incredible history? The story is full of surprises, from the way the Bible was written to how it's been kept (or "preserved") over thousands of years.

The ten facts that follow will show you just how incredible the Bible's history really is. . .and why **it's still the most important Book ever written!**

The grass dries up.
The flower loses its color.
But the Word of our God stands forever.
ISAIAH 40:8

#1: It Used to Take Years to Make One Bible

Before the printing press was invented in 1455, every Bible had to be copied by hand. That could take months or even years to finish a single copy.

#2: The Bible Has Been Protected Through History

People have tried to destroy the Bible many times, but God never let them succeed. His Word has survived every attack, so that we can read it today.

"Heaven and earth will pass away, but My words will not pass away."
MATTHEW 24:35

#3: The Bible Is the Best-Selling Book Ever

The Bible is the world's most important Book, in terms of the number printed. *Billions* of copies have been made.

#4: The Bible Was Written for Everyone

The Bible was written for all people, no matter where they live, how old they are, or what language they speak. That means the Bible was written for *you*.

> *This is what the LORD says: "Heaven is My throne, and the earth is My footstool. . . . My hand has made all those things, and all those things have been," says the LORD. "But I will look to this man, even to him who is poor and of a contrite spirit and who trembles at My word."*
>
> ISAIAH 66:1–2 SKJV

#5: The Bible Was Divided into Chapters and Verses Later

When the Bible was first written, it didn't have chapters and verses. Those were added about a thousand years ago to make it easier to read and find parts.

#6: The Bible Talks About Many Historical People and Events

The Bible mentions many Egyptian pharaohs, Roman emperors, and historical events that match what researchers later found to be correct.

#7: The Bible Was Written on Three Continents

Parts of the Bible were written in Asia, Africa, and Europe.

#8: The Bible Is the Most Translated Book in the World

The entire Bible has been translated into more than 750 languages. Parts of the Bible have been translated into more than 1,200 additional languages.

"Your blood has bought men for God from every family and from every language and from every kind of people and from every nation."
REVELATION 5:9

#9: The Bible Has Been Smuggled Into Secret Places

People have risked their lives to share the Bible where it is illegal to have and study God's Word.

#10: YOU Can Help Preserve God's Word

By reading, memorizing, and sharing the Bible, you're part of the amazing story of keeping God's Word alive in hearts everywhere.

He said to me, "Son of man, take all My words that I say to you into your heart, and hear with your ears. Then go to the Jews who have been taken away from their land. Go to the sons of your people. And if they listen or not, tell them, 'This is what the Lord God says.'"

EZEKIEL 3:10–11

Section Three

WHAT'S IN THE BIBLE?

THE BIBLE: GOD'S LIBRARY OF BOOKS

We saw earlier that **the Bible is more like a library than a single book.** The word *Bible* comes from the Greek word *biblia*, which means "books."

Here's how this library—the Bible—is organized:

Testaments

The Bible is divided into two main parts called *testaments*. The Old Testament and the New Testament are the two big sections of God's story.

Books

Within the Old and New Testament are 66 books. Some books are mainly stories, some contain songs, some are full of wise sayings, and some are personal letters. Each book has its own name—here they are, in order:

Genesis
Exodus
Leviticus
Numbers
Deuteronomy
Joshua
Judges
Ruth
1–2 Samuel
1–2 Kings
1–2 Chronicles ↗
Ezra
Nehemiah
Esther
Job
Psalms
Proverbs
Ecclesiastes
Song of Solomon
Isaiah
Jeremiah
Lamentations ↗
Ezekiel
Daniel
Hosea
Joel
Amos
Obadiah
Jonah
Micah
Nahum
Habakkuk
Zephaniah ↗

Haggai	Romans	Titus
Zechariah	1–2 Corinthians	Philemon
Malachi	Galatians	Hebrews
Matthew	Ephesians	James
Mark	Philippians	1–2 Peter
Luke	Colossians	1–3 John
John	1–2 Thessalonians	Jude
Acts ↗	1–2 Timothy ↗	Revelation

Chapters

Each book is divided into *chapters*. Chapters are the biggest sections of each book. When you look at your Bible, you'll see big numbers on nearly every page. Those numbers tell you which chapter you're reading. For example, if you open the book of Genesis and see a big 1, you're in Genesis chapter 1.

Verses

Each chapter is divided into small sections called *verses*. Verses are shorter sentences or groups of sentences, like this: "For God so loved the world that He gave His only Son. Whoever puts his trust in God's Son will not be lost but will have life that lasts forever." That is "John 3:16," which means you'll find it in the book of John, chapter 3, verse 16.

References

Put the book name, chapter, and verse numbers together and you have a *reference*: for example, John 3:16; Genesis 1:1; Revelation 22:20.

Why Is the Bible Organized This Way?

A long time ago, people realized it would be helpful to divide the Bible into smaller sections so everyone could find things more easily. Imagine trying to find a specific story or verse without any references—that could take a long time.

Today, your Bible is organized to help you understand God's story, one part at a time. It's like a puzzle where every piece fits perfectly to show God's love for you.

This book is designed to help you understand your Bible. But don't just read *about* the Bible—***read your Bible!*** Go ahead and explore this incredible library of God's books—it's full of wonderful truths for you to learn.

The Laws of the Lord are right, giving joy to the heart. The Word of the Lord is pure, giving light to the eyes.
PSALM 19:8

WHAT IS A GENRE?

Have you ever heard the word *genre*? It's pronounced JOHN-ruh.

Genre is just a fancy word that means a type of writing. Think about movies you've watched—some can be funny, some are exciting, and some might be even a little scary. The Bible is kind of like that too. It contains many different types of writing. **Each writing style helps tell the story of God in a special way.**

Let's take a look at some of the genres—or types of writing—in the Bible!

History (Old Testament)

This type of writing tells true stories of people and events from long ago. You'll find stories about kings, battles, and dangers, and how God rescued His people.

The Books: Genesis, Exodus, Leviticus, Numbers, Deuteronomy, Joshua, Judges, Ruth, 1–2 Samuel, 1–2 Kings, 1–2 Chronicles, Ezra, Nehemiah, Esther

Poetry

Poetry in the Bible is full of beautiful words, but not the kind of poems that rhyme. The Bible's poetry helps us understand God's love and express our own feelings to Him.

The Book: Psalms

Wisdom

Wisdom books are packed with good advice for living to please God. They're full of lessons about life, choices, and what's most important.

The Books: Job, Proverbs, Ecclesiastes, Song of Solomon

Prophecy (Old Testament)

These books include messages from God that were shared by prophets—special messengers who told people about God's plans and promises.

The Books: Isaiah, Jeremiah, Lamentations, Ezekiel, Daniel, Hosea, Joel, Amos, Obadiah, Jonah, Micah, Nahum, Habakkuk, Zephaniah, Haggai, Zechariah, Malachi

Gospels

The Gospels are the books that tell the story of Jesus' life on Earth—His birth, miracles, teachings, death, and resurrection.

The Books: Matthew, Mark, Luke, John

History (New Testament)

This type of writing tells the story of how the church began, after Jesus' death, resurrection, and return to heaven.

The Book: Acts

Epistles

"Epistles" are letters written by leaders like Paul to encourage and teach Christians about following Jesus.

The Books: Romans, 1–2 Corinthians, Galatians, Ephesians, Philippians, Colossians, 1–2 Thessalonians, 1–2 Timothy, Titus, Philemon, Hebrews, James, 1–2 Peter, 1–3 John, Jude

Prophecy (New Testament)

There's only one book of this kind in the New Testament. It describes visions of the future and God's ultimate plan for the world.

The Book: Revelation

Picking Favorites

Each genre is special. It shows us different parts of who God is and what He plans for us. Whether it's a story about a brave hero, a poem about God's greatness, or advice for living wisely, every word in the Bible works together to tell the greatest story ever—God's story!

He can use different parts of the Bible to teach you truth and help you grow closer to Him. Not one word of the Bible is ever wasted.

Think about It!

Which genre is most interesting to you? Why?

WHAT IS THE OLD TESTAMENT?

The Old Testament is the first big part of the Bible. It contains the first 39 books, from Genesis to Malachi. The Old Testament is packed full of treasures! **The Old Testament helps us understand who God is,** how much He loves us, and how all things point to Jesus. Here are some of the major ideas:

God's Creation

The Old Testament starts at the very beginning—literally. In Genesis, we learn how God created everything: our world, the sun and stars, animals and plants, even people. He made it all good because He wanted us to live in a healthy, beautiful world. Sadly, it wasn't long until people messed things up. By disobeying God, they sinned.

In the beginning God made from nothing the heavens and the earth.
GENESIS 1:1

And God made man in His own likeness. In the likeness of God He made him. He made both male and female. And God wanted good to come to them, saying, "Give birth to many. Grow in number. Fill the earth and rule over it."
GENESIS 1:27–28

The History of Israel

The Old Testament tells the story of God's special people, the nation called Israel. They were chosen by God to show the world how amazing He is. From Abraham to Moses to King David, we see how God cared for His people, even when they didn't always follow Him.

God called to him from inside the bush, saying, "Moses, Moses!" Moses answered, "Here I am." God said, "Do not come near. Take your shoes off your feet. For the place where you are standing is holy ground." He said also, "I am the God of your father, the God of Abraham, the God of Isaac, and the God of Jacob. . . . I have seen the suffering of My people in Egypt. I have heard their cry because of the men who make them work. I know how they suffer. So I have come down to save them from the power of the Egyptians. I will bring them out of that land to a good big land, to a land flowing with milk and honey."

EXODUS 3:4–8

The Law

God gave His people rules, called "the law," to help them know how to live. These rules weren't just about following orders—they were about loving God and other people. The Ten Commandments are a great example of this.

And you must love the Lord your God with all your heart and with all your soul and with all your strength.
DEUTERONOMY 6:5

Prophecies of a Coming Savior

One of the most exciting things about the Old Testament is how it points to Jesus! God promised to send a Savior to rescue His people from sin. Many of the prophets—like Isaiah and Micah—wrote about this amazing promise hundreds of years before Jesus was born in the town of Bethlehem.

The Old Testament is like the beginning of a giant adventure story. It sets the stage for everything that happens in the New Testament. Because God inspired the story, everything fits together in an amazing way.

"Bethlehem Ephrathah, you are too little to be among the family groups of Judah. But from you One will come who will rule for Me in Israel. His coming was planned long ago, from the beginning."
MICAH 5:2

WHAT IS THE NEW TESTAMENT?

The New Testament is the second part of the Bible, and it's the amazing story of Jesus.

Jesus is God—one member of the "Trinity" of God the Father, God the Son, and God the Holy Spirit. The three members of the Trinity have always been—there was never a time when God did not exist. After God created the world and people messed it up by sinning, Jesus came to earth to live and die as a man. His death on the cross paid the price for people's sin, and they could be saved just by believing in Him.

As the last 27 books of the Bible, **the New Testament tells of the incredible love of God** through Jesus. Each book in the New Testament helps us understand more about God's plan for the whole world.

Jesus came and said to them, "All power has been given to Me in heaven and on earth. Go and make followers of all the nations. Baptize them in the name of the Father and of the Son and of the Holy Spirit. Teach them to do all the things I have told you."

MATTHEW 28:18–20

Here are some of the big ideas in the New Testament:

The Life of Jesus

The New Testament starts with four books called *Gospels*: Matthew, Mark, Luke, and John. These books tell us all about Jesus—His birth, His miracles, His teachings, and His love for people. They also share the incredible story of how Jesus died on the cross and rose from the grave in order to save us. That is very good news—which is the meaning of the word *gospel*!

Jesus went on to all the towns and cities. He taught in their places of worship. He preached the Good News of the holy nation of God. He healed every sickness and disease the people had.

MATTHEW 9:35

The Early Church

When Jesus went back to heaven, He gave His followers a job. These *apostles* began sharing the good news about Jesus everywhere they went. The book of Acts tells the story of how the first churches were started and how people began to follow Jesus all over the world.

Then those who gladly received his word were baptized, and the same day about three thousand souls were added to them. And they continued steadfastly in the apostles' doctrine and fellowship and in the breaking of bread and in prayers.

ACTS 2:41–42 SKJV

Words of Encouragement

Many books in the New Testament are letters, written by people like Paul, Peter, and John. These letters were sent to churches and individual people to help them know how to live for Jesus. These letters teach us about loving God, loving others, and living in faith every day.

Do not let yourself get tired of doing good. If we do not give up, we will get what is coming to us at the right time.
GALATIANS 6:9

Remember to do good and help each other. Gifts like this please God.
HEBREWS 13:16

God's Big Plan

The last book of the New Testament, Revelation, is a peek at how God will one day make everything right again. It's a reminder that Jesus will come back to earth to make everything right. His love and goodness will win forever!

"See! I am coming soon. I am bringing with Me the reward I will give to everyone for what he has done. I am the First and the Last. I am the beginning and the end. Those who wash their clothes clean are happy (who are washed by the blood of the Lamb). They will have the right to go into the city through the gates. They will have the right to eat the fruit of the tree of life. . . . I am Jesus."

REVELATION 22:12–14, 16

The New Testament shows us that Jesus is the Savior we all need—it's only through Him that we can have a close relationship with God. The New Testament is full of hope, love, and teaching on how to please God. Every word is part of the greatest story ever told!

Rhyme It!

Sin and sadness pass away
when Jesus comes to save the day.

ACTIVITY:

Old Testament Or New Testament?

Think you've got your Bible facts straight? Let's put your knowledge to the test! Read each event below and decide if it happened in the Old Testament (O) or the New Testament (N).

Remember: The Old Testament tells the story of God's creation, the laws, the prophets, and the people before Jesus came. The New Testament is all about Jesus' life, the early church, and how we're called to live as Christians today.

Will you be a Bible expert who can tell the difference? Let's find out. Ready. . .set. . .go!

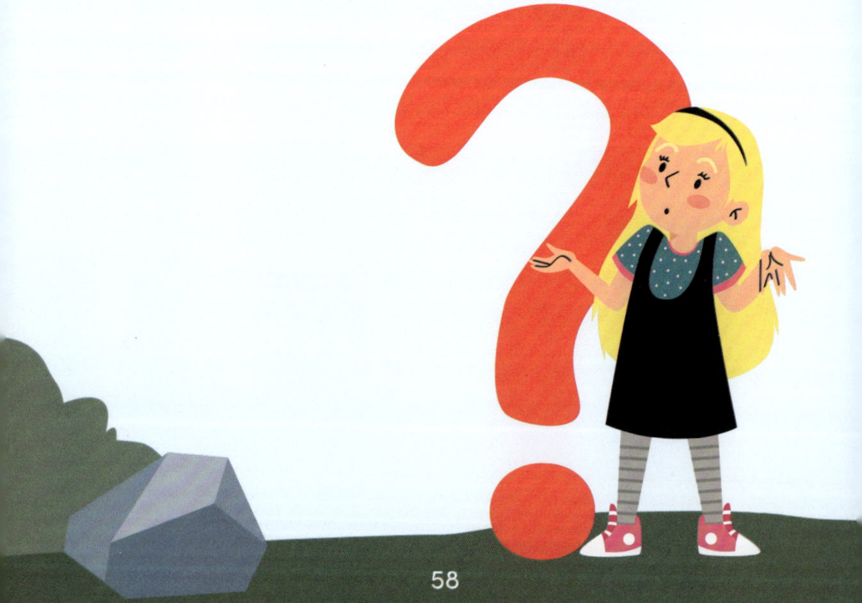

1. God created the world in six days. **O or N**

2. Jesus walked on water. **O or N**

3. Noah built an ark to save his family and the animals from a flood. **O or N**

4. Moses received the Ten Commandments. **O or N**

5. Jesus healed a blind man. **O or N**

6. Jonah was swallowed by a big fish. **O or N**

7. David defeated the giant Goliath with a sling and a stone. **O or N**

8. The angel Gabriel told Mary she would give birth to Jesus. **O or N**

9. Jesus fed 5,000 people with five loaves and two fish. **O or N**

10. Daniel was thrown into the lions' den, but God kept him safe. **O or N**

11. God parted the Red Sea so the Israelites could escape from Egypt. **O or N**

12. Joseph's brothers sold him into slavery in Egypt. **O or N**

13. Zacchaeus climbed a tree to see Jesus. **O or N**

14. Esther became queen and helped save her people. **O or N**

15. Saul (later called Paul) met Jesus on the road to Damascus. **O or N**

16. The walls of Jericho came crumbling down. **O or N**

17. Deborah served as a judge and military leader of God's people. **O or N**

18. Jesus turned water into wine. **O or N**

19. Elijah defeated 450 prophets of the false god Baal. **O or N**

20. Judas Iscariot betrayed Jesus for thirty pieces of silver. **O or N**

21. Shadrach, Meshach, and Abednego survived a trip to the fiery furnace. **O or N**

How do you think you did? Are you able to tell the difference between the Old and New Testaments? On the next page, let's see how many you got right.

Answers

1. O	7. O	13. N	19. O
2. N	8. N	14. O	20. N
3. O	9. N	15. N	21. O
4. O	10. O	16. O	
5. N	11. O	17. O	
6. O	12. O	18. N	

Scoring

0–7 Correct: Bible Beginner
You're just getting started! Keep reading and learning more about God's amazing story. You're off to a great start.

8–14 Correct: Bible Detective
You're paying attention and uncovering the truth about the Bible's big events. Great job!

15–21 Correct: Bible Expert
You know a lot about God's Word! You're like a walking, talking Bible encyclopedia. Keep it up!

Section Four

WHAT'S THE BIBLE ABOUT?

THE BIG PICTURE: GOD'S STORY

The Bible is *not* just a bunch of random stories thrown together. **The Bible is one big story**—a story that tells us about God and how He has worked through history. All the different parts of the Bible work together to tell a single amazing story. It's the "big picture" of how God created everything, how people turned away from Him, and how He made a way to bring us back to Himself through Jesus.

Here's how it all fits together:

In the beginning, God created the world and everything in it. He made us to have a special relationship with Him.

Then God said, "Let Us make man like Us and let him be head over the fish of the sea, and over the birds of the air, and over the cattle, and over all the earth, and over every thing that moves on the ground."
GENESIS 1:26

But people made choices that hurt that relationship. Sin entered the world, and the Bible shows us the consequences.

This is what happened: Sin came into the world by one man, Adam. Sin brought death with it. Death spread to all men because all have sinned.

ROMANS 5:12

God didn't leave us! He promised a Savior who would come to fix everything. This Savior is Jesus!

See, the Lord has made it known to the end of the earth: Say to the people of Zion, "Look, the One Who saves you is coming! See, He is bringing His reward that He will give."

ISAIAH 62:11

Through Jesus, God showed us His love. He made it possible for us to be close to Him again. Jesus' death and resurrection were the greatest part of God's plan!

He gave the right and the power to become children of God to those who received Him. He gave this to those who put their trust in His name.

JOHN 1:12

Jesus will come back to make everything perfect again. And then He will rule forever as King of the universe.

> *At the end of the world, Christ will give His holy nation over to God the Father. Christ will have destroyed every nation and power. Christ must be King until He has destroyed all those who hate Him and work against Him. The last thing that will be destroyed is death. The Holy Writings say that God has put all things under Christ's feet except Himself. When Christ is over all things, He will put Himself under God Who put all things under Christ. And God will be over all things.*
>
> 1 CORINTHIANS 15:24–28

All of the books in the Bible, from Genesis to Revelation, tell parts of this incredible story. Every part points to God's love for us and His plan to rescue us. It's like a giant puzzle, but when we put it all together, we see God's big story. And we get to be part of it!

Now let's look a little closer at some of these key ideas throughout God's big story.

GOD AND PEOPLE: HIS LOVE FOR YOU

Did you know that God loves you more than anyone else ever could? From the very beginning, He created people because He wanted to have a special relationship with us. He didn't just make people and leave us alone. **God made us to enjoy friendship with Him,** to talk with Him, and to care for the world He created.

The Lord came to us from far away, saying, "I have loved you with a love that lasts forever. So I have helped you come to Me with loving-kindness."
JEREMIAH 31:3

See what great love the Father has for us that He would call us His children. And that is what we are. For this reason the people of the world do not know who we are because they did not know Him. Dear friends, we are God's children now. But it has not yet been shown to us what we are going to be. We know that when He comes again, we will be like Him because we will see Him as He is.
1 JOHN 3:1–2

God's love for you is huge!

It's the kind of love that never goes away, no matter what. In fact, the Bible tells us that God loves us so much that He sent His Son, Jesus, to die on the cross for our sins. The perfect man—God in a human body—paid the price for every wrong thing we've ever done. This shows just how far God would go to be close to you. Jesus' life and sacrifice on the cross are the biggest possible proof of God's love.

Now, **God wants you to love Him back.** And He wants you to love other people too. When we love God and love others, we show the world just how awesome God really is.

We love Him because He loved us first.
1 JOHN 4:19

"I [Jesus] give you a new Law. You are to love each other. You must love each other as I have loved you. If you love each other, all men will know you are My followers."
JOHN 13:34–35

Even when we make mistakes or mess up, God still loves us. He still wants us to be close to Him. God is always ready to forgive us and help us make things right.

For I know that nothing can keep us from the love of God. Death cannot! Life cannot! Angels cannot! Leaders cannot! Any other power cannot! Hard things now or in the future cannot! The world above or the world below cannot! Any other living thing cannot keep us away from the love of God which is ours through Christ Jesus our Lord.

ROMANS 8:38–39

The Bible says that *nothing* can separate us from God's love. Not even:

Bad days. Even when we're feeling down or frustrated, God still loves us.

Mess-ups. No matter how many times we mess up, God will always love us and help us do better.

Big changes. Whether you move to a new place or your life changes in some other huge way, God's love will stay the same.

Not winning. Win or lose, God still loves you with the same big love.

God's love for you isn't based on how good you are. It's not based on what you do. If you follow Jesus, God's love toward you will not change, no matter what. You can always trust that He loves you—forever and ever!

HOW SIN CAME INTO THE WORLD. . . AND WHAT JESUS DID TO FIX IT

A long time ago, in the beginning of time, everything was just right. God made the world and everything in it, and He said it was all very good. He made people to love Him and have a close friendship with Him. But one day, something went wrong.

The first people made a bad choice. **Adam and Eve disobeyed God** and ate some fruit that God had told them not to eat. This was the first *sin*. Things weren't perfect anymore. Sin was now part of the world. People started doing things that hurt themselves, others, and God.

Then the Lord saw that man was very sinful on the earth. Every plan and thought of the heart of man was sinful always. The Lord was sorry that He had made man on the earth. He had sorrow in His heart.

GENESIS 6:5–6

Sin is doing anything that goes against what God wants. Lying is sin. Being unkind is sin. Stealing is sin. Thinking any kind of bad thoughts is sin. And **sin separates people from God.**

Sadly, every single person in the world is affected by sin. No one can fix it by themselves.

Everyone has turned away from God.
They have all done wrong. Not one of them
does what is good. No, not even one!
ROMANS 3:12

But God didn't want to people to be stuck in their sins. The Father sent Jesus, His Son, into the world to fix what sin broke. Jesus became a man—a human being like all of us. He lived a perfect life, showing us what God's love looks like.

But even though Jesus never sinned, He died on the cross for sin—*our* sin. That's how much Jesus loves people! When He died, **Jesus took the punishment for every sin** that every person has done. And then Jesus did another amazing thing—He came back to life! This "resurrection" showed us that God is stronger than anything, even death.

Now, anyone who believes in Jesus can be right with God. Jesus made the way for people to be saved from their sin and its punishment. God wants every person to "accept" Jesus into their life. That means we need to believe Jesus is God's Son. . .that He became a man who died on the cross for sins. . .and that He came back to life to prove His incredible power. When we do that, we are "saved from sin." And then Jesus helps us to live in a way that pleases God.

If you say with your mouth that Jesus is Lord, and believe in your heart that God raised Him from the dead, you will be saved from the punishment of sin.

ROMANS 10:9

Jesus fixed what sin broke so that we can be close to God forever!

When you believe that Jesus is Lord and that God raised Him from the dead, you can experience this incredible gift of friendship with God. It's not about being perfect or doing enough good things—it's about believing in Jesus and trusting Him to forgive you.

Jesus made it possible for us to come close to God. **Our belief in Jesus allows us to be God's children!** That is the best news ever.

You should not act like people who are owned by someone. They are always afraid. Instead, the Holy Spirit makes us His sons, and we can call to Him, "My Father."
ROMANS 8:15

HOW TO FOLLOW JESUS

When you learn the Bible, you learn that Jesus wants you to be part of His family forever. If you trust Him, He promises to always be with you. On this earth, Jesus will walk with you every step of the way. Then He'll give you *eternal* life—a perfect life that never ends—with Him. You'll get to live with God not just now, but forever! How amazing is that?

Jesus wants you to follow Him. What exactly does that mean? It's really as easy as A-B-C:

Admit that you've made wrong choices (called *sin*) and ask God to forgive you.

Believe that Jesus died on the cross for your sins and rose again to give you new life.

Choose to live for Jesus every day by obeying Him.

Remember!

A-B-C = Admit, Believe, Choose

A Forever Friendship

When you follow Jesus, it's the beginning of the best friendship ever. He is always with you, helping, guiding, and loving you. And when your life on earth is over, you'll get to live with Him forever in heaven.

> *"Do not let your heart be troubled. You have put your trust in God, put your trust in Me also. There are many rooms in My Father's house. If it were not so, I would have told you. I am going away to make a place for you. After I go and make a place for you, I will come back and take you with Me. Then you may be where I am."*
>
> JOHN 14:1–3

Isn't it exciting to know that Jesus made a way for us to be with Him forever? Life with Jesus is the greatest adventure. . .and it lasts for all eternity!

What Happens When You Follow Jesus?

Following Jesus is the best, smartest, happiest choice you can ever make in life. Here are some of the great things that happen when you become a Christian:

You're forgiven! Jesus forgives you completely when you ask. He washes away your sins and gives you a fresh start.

You become part of God's family. Nothing can separate you from His love!

You can talk to God anytime. Following Jesus means you have a direct connection to God. You can pray to Him about anything—big or small—and He promises to listen.

You have a new purpose. God helps you live in a way that honors Him.

You can grow closer to God every day. Reading the Bible, praying, and worshiping God help you know Him better and see how much He loves you. The closer you get to Him, the more exciting your journey with Jesus becomes.

You have hope. Even when life is hard, following Jesus gives you hope. Why? Because you know God is always in control and has a good plan for you.

You'll live forever with Jesus. Following Jesus isn't just for today—it's for forever. Your friendship with Him starts now and lasts for eternity!

For by His loving-favor you have been saved from the punishment of sin through faith. It is not by anything you have done. It is a gift of God.
EPHESIANS 2:8

Thank God for His great Gift.
2 CORINTHIANS 9:15

ACTIVITY:

Bible Verses to Remember

The Bible is packed with amazing verses to remind you of God's big story. These verses tell of His love for you and how you can live with Him forever.

Following are some verses to memorize and keep in your heart. They'll help you understand the incredible things God has done for you!

In the beginning God made from nothing
the heavens and the earth.
GENESIS 1:1

(This verse reminds us that God started it all—
He made the world and everything in it!)

We love Him because He loved us first.
1 JOHN 4:19

(God made you to love you, and He loves
you because He made you. He wants a
relationship with you that lasts forever!)

This is what happened: Sin came into the world by one man, Adam. Sin brought death with it. Death spread to all men because all have sinned.
ROMANS 5:12

(When Adam and Eve disobeyed God, sin entered the world. Because of sin, everyone needs God's help. But, thankfully, God didn't leave us stuck in our mess. He sent Jesus to save us!)

This is love! It is not that we loved God but that He loved us. For God sent His Son to pay for our sins with His own blood.
1 JOHN 4:10

(This is the greatest rescue plan ever. Jesus gave His own life so that we could live forever with Him.)

Jesus said, "I am the Way and the Truth and the Life. No one can go to the Father except by Me."
JOHN 14:6

(Trusting Jesus is the only way to know God and live with Him forever. He is the truth we can trust, our one source of hope.)

"For sure, I tell you, he who puts his trust in Me has life that lasts forever."
JOHN 6:47

(When you follow Jesus, you become part of God's family, *forever*!)

Fun Tip for Memorizing

Memorizing God's Word is one of the wisest things you can do. And it's easier than you think. Pick just one verse each week to learn. Write it down on a piece of paper or a note card. Use colorful pens, draw pictures around it, sketch out a related scene—anything to make it stand out in your brain. Then read and re-read your verse throughout the day. Challenge yourself to say it back without looking.

Try posting your verse in places where you'll see it often—on your mirror, in your locker, or by your desk. The more you see the verse, the more it will stick in your heart and mind.

Before you know it, you'll have a whole collection of Bible verses hidden in your heart!

"Keep these words of mine in your heart and in your soul."
DEUTERONOMY 11:18

Section Five

WHAT BIBLE STORIES SHOULD EVERYONE KNOW?

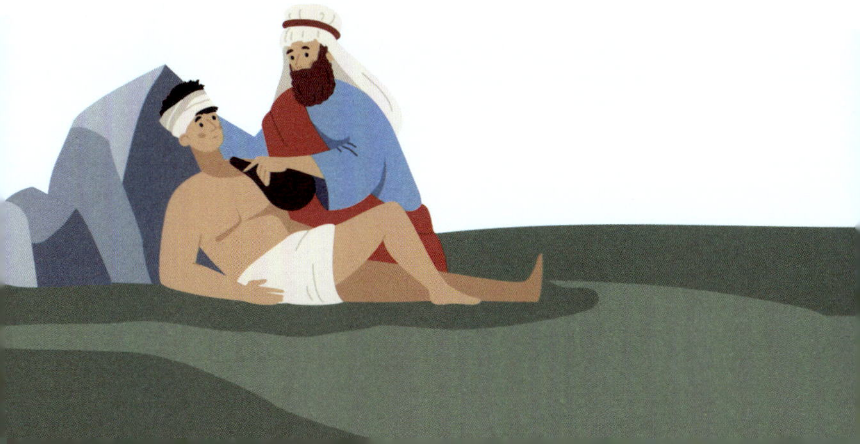

CREATION: THE BEGINNING OF EVERYTHING (GENESIS 1)

In the very beginning, before anything else existed, God created the world. **God just spoke words,** and the earth and sky and oceans—and everything in them—came into being. With each step, God said it was good.

God's most amazing creation was people. He made Adam and Eve in His own image. That means they were like God in many ways, able to think and speak and love. God wanted them to live with Him in His beautiful world.

Everything was just right. The world was full of life, with trees and flowers, butterflies and giraffes and goldfish. But the best part of creation was people, who could enjoy God's presence with them.

God saw all that He had made and it was very good. There was evening and there was morning, the sixth day.
GENESIS 1:31

God's creation shows His love for *you*!

Men cannot say they do not know about God. From the beginning of the world, men could see what God is like through the things He has made. This shows His power that lasts forever. It shows that He is God.
ROMANS 1:20

Trust in the living God, who richly gives us all things to enjoy.
1 TIMOTHY 6:17 SKJV

God made everything in just six days! Imagine all that happened in that one week.

Let's take a quick look at what God created.

Day 1: He made light, separating day from night.

Day 2: He created the sky, separating the waters above from the waters below.

Day 3: He gathered water into seas and made dry land, filling it with plants.

Day 4: He made the sun, moon, and stars to give light to the world.

Day 5: He created birds and fish.

Day 6: He made animals and, finally, *people*. Adam and Eve were expected to care for the earth.

Day 7: He rested, enjoying His perfect creation. Everything God made was good, and He made us to enjoy it with Him!

God's creation is incredible—and He made it all for us. From the stars in the sky to the plants on the earth, everything God made was good.

Think about It!

Which day of creation is your favorite, and why?

NOAH'S ARK: GOD'S BIG RESCUE (GENESIS 6-8)

This special story from the Bible tells how God saved Noah, his family, and many animals from a huge flood. They escaped the water in a big boat called the "ark."

A long time ago, because of sin, the world had become a very bad place. People weren't following God at all, except for a man named Noah and his family. **Noah loved God and obeyed God's Word.** So God told Noah that He was going to send a flood to clean up the earth. Noah should build a huge boat that would protect him and his family—and many animals. Everything else would be destroyed by the flood.

God looked at the earth and saw how sinful it was. For all who lived on the earth had become sinful in their ways. Then God said to Noah, "I have decided to make an end to all the people on the earth. They are the cause of very much trouble. See, I will destroy them as I destroy the earth. Make a large boat of gopher wood for yourself."

GENESIS 6:12–14

Noah spent many years building that huge ark. Then, when God told him it was time, Noah brought two of every kind of animal—birds, lions, elephants, all of them—into the ark with him. It started to rain, and it rained and rained and rained. After forty days and nights of rain, the ark was floating safely on the water.

After many months, the flood waters went down. The ark landed in a place called Ararat. Noah and the animals stepped out to begin a new life on earth.

God promised never to flood the earth again. And He put a rainbow in the sky as the sign of His promise.

"When I bring clouds over the earth and the rain-bow is seen in the clouds, I will remember My agreement that is between Me and you and every living thing of all flesh. Never again will the water become a flood to destroy all flesh."

GENESIS 9:14–15

Fun Facts about the Story of Noah's Ark

A super-sized boat: The ark was about 450 feet long and 75 feet wide, which is bigger than a football field. It was 45 feet high, about as tall as a five-story building.

A big storm: It rained for 40 days and nights—imagine heavy, non-stop rain for over a month. The water covered the whole earth for five months.

A bunch of animals: The Bible says Noah took two of every kind of animal, but for some "clean" animals (the ones that were good for sacrifices), he brought seven pairs.

Think about It!

What do you think it was like traveling on a floating zoo?

A fresh start. After the flood, Noah and his family were the only people left on earth. They got to start over with God's blessing.

A promise for us. After the flood, God placed a rainbow in the sky as a promise that He would never again destroy the earth by water. Today, the rainbow reminds us that God keeps His promises. We can always trust Him.

The story of Noah's ark teaches many valuable lessons. We learn the importance of obeying God, the fact that God can't stand evil, and the truth that He always keeps His promises.

Jesus says yes to all of God's many promises. It is through Jesus that we say, "Let it be so," when we give thanks to God.
2 CORINTHIANS 1:20

DAVID AND GOLIATH: THE SHEPHERD BOY WHO DEFEATED A GIANT (1 SAMUEL 17)

Goliath was a giant enemy soldier who scared everyone in the land of Israel. He kept calling for the Israelite army to send a man to fight him. But no one was brave enough to face this huge warrior.

But then a young shepherd named David showed up. He visited the Israelite army to deliver food to his older brothers. When he heard Goliath shouting insults, he was filled with faith. "I can fight him!" David said. "God will help me!" **The young man trusted God's Word,** even though he was much smaller than Goliath and had no armor to protect himself.

David said to the Philistine, "You come to me with a sword and spears. But I come to you in the name of the Lord of All, the God of the armies of Israel, Whom you have stood against. This day the Lord will give you into my hands. I will knock you down and cut off your head. This day I will give the dead bodies of the army of the Philistines to the birds of the sky and the wild animals of the earth. Then all the earth may know that there is a God in Israel."

1 SAMUEL 17:45–46

David didn't even have a sword. He just took a sling and a handful of smooth stones. As Goliath stomped toward him, David put one stone in his sling and swung it around and around. When he let it go, the stone flew straight into Goliath's forehead! He fell down to the ground, and David used the giant's own sword to kill him. David could only do these things because he trusted in God.

David said. . . , "All these people gathered here may know that the Lord does not save with sword and spear. For the battle is the Lord's and He will give you into our hands."

1 SAMUEL 17:45, 47

David's courageous faith showed everyone that *God* is powerful, no matter how big our challenge.

Fun Facts about the Story of David and Goliath

Goliath was more than nine feet tall. His head would have almost touched the bottom of a basketball hoop.

David didn't wear any protective armor. King Saul offered his armor to protect David from Goliath, but it was too big and heavy. In faith, David went without.

David used a sling and a stone. Instead of a sword and shield, David used a sling and five smooth stones he picked up from a stream.

David only needed *one* stone. Though he had five with him, the first stone hit Goliath right in the forehead, knocking the giant to the ground.

The battle wasn't about strength. David trusted God to help him win, showing that faith is more important than anything else.

David would later become a king. The boy who defeated Goliath later became Israel's greatest ruler.

David could defeat the giant Goliath because the battle belonged to God. David's size, strength, and skill weren't the important things—it was David's God. The Lord will always win the battles He fights, no matter how big or impossible they seem to us.

The Lord says to you, "Do not be afraid or troubled because of these many men. For the battle is not yours but God's."
2 CHRONICLES 20:15

THE FIRST CHRISTMAS: A KING IS BORN

A long time ago, God made a special promise to send a Savior to the world. That Savior was Jesus. The story of His birth is wonderful and exciting.

A young woman named Mary was engaged to be married. She loved Joseph, who would become her husband, and she loved God. God loved Mary too, and He had a very important job for her. **God sent an angel to tell Mary that she would have a baby.** But she wouldn't have this baby with Joseph—Mary's baby would be the Son of God!

Mary became pregnant, just as God had said. When it was nearly time for the baby to be born, the government ordered everyone to go to the places their families had come from. So Mary and Joseph traveled to the little town of Bethlehem. There was no room at the inn for them, so they slept in a place where animals were kept. And that night, Mary had her baby, Jesus, who would grow up to save the world. On this night, though, she wrapped Him in cloths and laid Him in a manger—a feeding trough for animals.

The angel said to them, "Do not be afraid. See! I bring you good news of great joy which is for all people. Today, One Who saves from the punishment of sin has been born in the city of David. He is Christ the Lord."

LUKE 2:10–11

Five Things to Know about the Birth of Jesus

Jesus is God's Son. Jesus wasn't just an ordinary baby—He is God's Son, sent to save us! Jesus' birth was part of God's big, wonderful plan to rescue people from sin.

It happened just as God promised. Long before Jesus was born, the Bible said the Savior would come. Prophets wrote about it, and God's promises came true!

For to us a Child will be born. To us a Son will be given. And the rule of the nations will be on His shoulders. His name will be called Wonderful, Teacher, Powerful God, Father Who Lives Forever, Prince of Peace. There will be no end to His rule and His peace, upon the throne of David and over his nation. He will build it to last and keep it strong with what is right and fair and good from that time and forever. The work of the Lord of All will do this.

ISAIAH 9:6–7

He came to earth in a humble way. Jesus, the King of Kings, wasn't born in a palace. He was born in a stable and laid in a manger.

God chose ordinary people to be part of His story. God chose regular people like shepherds to be the first to learn of Jesus' birth.

Jesus was born for everyone. Jesus didn't come to earth to help just the important people—He came for *all* of us. The shepherds, the wise men, and everyone who heard the news of His birth were invited to know and worship Him.

Then Peter said, "I can see, for sure, that God does not respect one person more than another. He is pleased with any man in any nation who honors Him and does what is right."
ACTS 10:34–35

Think about It!

Are you one of those kids who honors God and does what is right?

THE RESURRECTION: JESUS IS ALIVE!

After Jesus died on the cross, His friends were very sad. They placed His body in a tomb and rolled a big stone in front of it. They had placed all of their hope and trust in Jesus. But now He was dead.

On the third day, though, something amazing happened.

Early that morning, some of Jesus' friends went to the tomb. But when they arrived, they found that the stone had been rolled away. . .and the tomb was empty!

A brightly shining angel appeared to Jesus' friends. He told them:

"He is not here! He has risen from the dead as He said He would."
MATTHEW 28:6

Jesus had come back to life, just as He promised He would. His friends were so happy and excited! They saw Jesus alive again, and **He told them to go share this good news with everyone.**

Jesus' resurrection shows us that He has power over death. That proves that we can live forever with Him. By His death on the cross, Jesus took the punishment for sin. And when He came back to life, He showed it was possible for us to have a forever friendship with God.

Jesus said, "I am the Way and the Truth and the Life. No one can go to the Father except by Me."
JOHN 14:6

Now that we have been made right with God by putting our trust in Him, we have peace with Him. It is because of what our Lord Jesus Christ did for us. By putting our trust in God, He has given us His loving-favor and has received us. We are happy for the hope we have of sharing the shining-greatness of God.
ROMANS 5:1–2

Why Does the Resurrection Matter?

The resurrection of Jesus is the most important event in history! It's not just something we celebrate at Easter time—it's the reason we have hope and joy throughout our lives.

When Jesus rose from the dead, He proved that He is stronger than anything, even death itself! So why does the Resurrection matter so much?

If the dead are not raised, then not even Christ was raised from the dead. If Christ was not raised from the dead, your faith is worth nothing and you are still living in your sins. Then the Christians who have already died are lost in sin. If we have hope in Christ in this life only, we are more sad than anyone else. But it is true! Christ has been raised from the dead! He was the first One to be raised from the dead and all those who are in graves will follow.

1 CORINTHIANS 15:16–20

Let's take a look at some important reasons why Jesus' resurrection changes everything:

Jesus conquered death. He didn't stay dead! His resurrection shows us that Jesus has power over all things.

Jesus proved He is God's Son. Jesus' resurrection proves that He truly is who He said He was—the only Son of God, sent to save us.

We can receive eternal life with God. Because Jesus came back to life, He has the power to offer us eternal life with Him. All He asks is our faith in Him.

If you say with your mouth that Jesus is Lord, and believe in your heart that God raised Him from the dead, you will be saved from the punishment of sin.

ROMANS 10:9

God keeps His promises. Jesus said He would rise again, and He did! This proves that God keeps His promises. We can trust Him.

Jesus is our hope. The Resurrection gives us the confidence that God has power to make everything right—no matter how hard things might seem right now.

The resurrection of Jesus changes everything! It shows us that death is not the end, and we can have new life through Him. Because Jesus is alive, we have hope and the promise of eternal life with God—forever.

Anything is possible. Nothing is too hard for God!

When His followers heard this, they could not understand it. They said, "Then who can be saved from the punishment of sin?" Jesus looked at them and said, "This cannot be done by men. But with God all things can be done."

MATTHEW 19:25–26

Section Six

HOW DO I READ MY BIBLE?

GETTING STARTED: YOUR GUIDE TO BIBLE ADVENTURE

Reading your Bible is like discovering a treasure chest. God's Word is full of amazing stories, exciting promises, and much-needed wisdom. Here are some tips to help you **start reading the Bible for yourself:**

Choose a Bible that you can understand. Ask your mom or dad, or your pastor or Sunday school teacher to help you find a version that uses simple, clear words.

Pray before you start reading. Ask God to help you understand what you're reading. Remember—He wrote the Bible! Pray for Him to speak to your heart through His Word.

If you do not have wisdom, ask God for it. He is always ready to give it to you and will never say you are wrong for asking. You must have faith as you ask Him. You must not doubt. Anyone who doubts is like a wave which is pushed around by the sea.

JAMES 1:5–6

Start reading in the New Testament. Specifically, start with the Gospels. The first four books in the New Testament—Matthew, Mark, Luke, and John—are a great place to begin. They tell the story of Jesus.

Read a little each day. You don't have to read the whole Bible at one time. Start with a small section—maybe one chapter or even a few verses—and take your time. The goal isn't to read a lot fast, but to read just enough that you can really understand and learn from.

Ask questions. When something doesn't make sense, talk to an adult you trust—like your parent, teacher, or pastor. They can help to explain confusing parts of the Bible.

He who is taught God's Word should share the good things he has with his teacher.
GALATIANS 6:6

More Advice for New Bible Readers

Here's a little more advice to help you keep reading your Bible, once you've gotten started:

Be consistent. Try to read something from your Bible every day, even if it's just a few verses. The more you read, the more you'll grow.

Keep going. Sometimes the Bible can be hard to understand, but keep reading! God will help you understand when the time is right.

Take notes or draw. Use your hands as well as your eyes when you read. It may help you to remember important truths.

"Each of you take up a stone on his shoulder, according to the number of the tribes of the children of Israel, that this may be a sign among you when your children ask their fathers in the future, saying, 'What do you mean by these stones?' Then you shall answer them that the waters of the Jordan were cut off before the ark of the covenant of the LORD. When it crossed over the Jordan, the waters of the Jordan were cut off. And these stones shall be a memorial to the children of Israel forever."

JOSHUA 4:5–7 SKJV

Take breaks. If you miss a day or get overwhelmed, don't feel bad! Just pick up where you left off and keep going. Ask God for help. He's always patient with you.

Share what you're learning. What you're doing is exciting! Share a Bible verse or story with a friend or family member. Don't be afraid to tell people what you find in God's Word.

Always pray. We mentioned this before, but it's so important that we'll say it again. The Bible is not just a book—it's God's way of talking to you. Listen, learn, and *talk to Him* about what you read.

The person who is not a Christian does not understand these words from the Holy Spirit. He thinks they are foolish. He cannot understand them because he does not have the Holy Spirit to help him understand.

1 CORINTHIANS 2:14

HOW TO DIG DEEPER IN YOUR BIBLE

When you're learning your Bible, it can help to ask yourself some important questions to really understand what God is saying.

Following are a few questions to think about as you read:

Question:

What is the main point of this passage?

Sometimes a verse or story can be hard to understand. Ask yourself, "What is the most important thing God seems to be saying here?"

Question:

What does my reading tell me about God?

Look for clues about who God is and what He's like. You can learn something about God on every single page of your Bible if you look.

The Lord is good to all. And His loving-kindness is over all His works.
PSALM 145:9

Question:

What does my reading teach me about people?

Think about how the people in the story or Bible passage act. What can you learn from their choices?

Question:

How can I apply this to my life?

God's Word isn't just a story—it's meant to help us love God and live better. Think about how you can use what you read to make better choices.

Obey the Word of God. If you hear only and do not act, you are only fooling yourself. Anyone who hears the Word of God and does not obey is like a man looking at his face in a mirror. After he sees himself and goes away, he forgets what he looks like.

JAMES 1:22–24

Let's Practice: Digging Deeper in Your Bible

The Bible is full of life-changing stories that teach us about God's love and how we should behave. One of those stories is about a man named Zacchaeus. He wasn't very popular—he was a tax collector who often took more money than he should have. But when Jesus came to town, Zacchaeus' life changed forever.

Let's use the questions we just learned to dig deeper into the story of Zacchaeus. . .and see what God wants us to learn!

Look up Luke 19 in your Bible or online, if that's okay with your parents.

Question:

What is the main point of this passage?

Jesus came to seek and save everyone, no matter who they are or what they've done.

Question:

What does my reading tell me about God?

God is loving and forgiving. God sees our hearts and knows when we want to change. Just like Jesus reached out to Zacchaeus, God wants people to know Him, no matter who they are or what they've done. God's kindness leads us to live in a way that honors Him.

Question:

What does my reading teach me about people?

People can change. Zacchaeus started out as someone who was selfish and dishonest, but when he met Jesus, he wanted to live differently. Nobody is too far gone for Jesus to love or forgive.

Question:

How can I apply this to my life?

Like Zacchaeus, we should be willing to make changes when we realize we've done something wrong. We can also practice kindness and generosity, just like Zacchaeus did after meeting Jesus.

WHAT HAPPENS WHEN I DON'T UNDERSTAND A VERSE?

When you don't understand a verse, don't worry—it happens to everyone! **The Bible is full of big ideas,** and some parts take time to understand.

Here's what you can do to get over that obstacle:

Pray and ask God for help. God wants you to understand His Word, so ask Him to teach you.

Ask for help from a trusted adult. A parent, teacher, or pastor might be able to explain the verse or verses you don't understand.

Look for the big picture. Even if one verse is tricky, think about what the whole story or chapter is about.

Keep at it. You might not understand everything right away, but keep reading and learning—you'll grow little by little!

Remember, learning the Bible is not a race. It's okay if you don't understand everything the first time you read a verse or passage. The more you read, pray, and talk with others, the more you'll understand. Keep asking questions, of adults and of God Himself. Know that He is always with you, helping you to learn more about Him every day.

Show me Your ways, O Lord. Teach me Your paths. Lead me in Your truth and teach me. For You are the God Who saves me. I wait for You all day long.
PSALM 25:4–5

Teach me Your way, O Lord. I will walk in Your truth. May my heart fear Your name.
PSALM 86:11

Let's Be Bible Detectives!

Sometimes, verses can feel like a puzzle we can't quite put together. But every good detective knows that if they stay on the case, they can solve the mystery.

Here's how to start your detective work when you don't understand a verse:

Look for clues. What's happening in the verses around your reading? Sometimes the overall story (or the verses before and after the one you're reading) can help to make the meaning clear.

Ask the experts. Who in your life can be like a "Bible mentor" to you? Maybe a parent, an older sibling, a teacher, or pastor can help.

Use your Bible tools. Your Bible might have footnotes (information at the bottom of each page), cross references (related chapter-and-verse details in the margins), or even maps in the back to help explain things.

Don't give up! Keep reading and investigating. If you can't find the answer you need, write the question down so you can remember to ask someone later. It may take time to find the answer to your question—but trust that God will help you find it in His good time.

Do not let yourselves get tired of doing good. If we do not give up, we will get what is coming to us at the right time.
GALATIANS 6:9

A Prayer for Learning the Bible!

Lord God, I want to know Your Word better. Since You wrote it, will You please help me to understand it? I want to know what You've said and live my life in obedience. Thank You!

WHAT SHOULD I READ?

There are lots of great Bible reading plans you can choose from. Which one is best? The one you'll actually stick with and use!

Here are a few simple Bible reading plans to help you learn the Bible:

Read one chapter each day. Pick a book of the Bible (like Psalms, Proverbs, or Matthew) and read a chapter every day.

Interesting Idea!

The book of Proverbs has 31 chapters and most months have 31 days. So a lot of people like to read one chapter of Proverbs on the matching day of the month. That means they read Proverbs 1 on the first day of the month, Proverbs 2 on the second day, and so on. It's an easy way to keep track of your progress.

Study a verse a day. Instead of tackling a whole chapter, pick just one verse to focus on each day. Write it down. Memorize it. Think how the verse speaks to your own life. Write out a short prayer to God about what you've read.

Happy is the man [or woman, boy, or girl] who does not walk in the way sinful men tell him to, or stand in the path of sinners, or sit with those who laugh at the truth. But he finds joy in the Law of the Lord and thinks about His Law day and night.

PSALM 1:1–2

Focus on a theme. You can study different topics in the Bible by searching for verses that are related. Bible themes include honesty, knowing God, hard work, hope, loneliness, and many more. You can ask a trusted adult for help with finding verses on a theme. (By the way, the book of Proverbs is packed with great Bible themes.)

Here's an example of how to focus on a theme:

Honesty

Proverbs 12:17

Proverbs 12:22

Proverbs 14:25

Proverbs 21:6

Proverbs 24:26

So, what does the Bible have to say about lying? Why is telling the truth important to God?

Jesus said, "I am. . .the Truth."
JOHN 14:6

Read the Bible in a year. If you're ready for a *big* challenge, try reading through the whole Bible in a year. At the end of this book, starting on page 124, you'll find one plan that might take 20–30 minutes each day for a year. There are many other reading plans online or in Bible apps.

Important Point!

No matter how you choose to learn the Bible, the most important thing is to keep at it. As you read and study, you'll be learning more about God. And nothing is more important than that!

O, how I love Your Law! It is what I think about all through the day.
PSALM 119:97

If you ever find that your Bible reading plan really isn't working for you, that's okay. If it's too hard to keep up with, just try a new one. The important thing is that you don't stop reading the Bible! Keep at it until you find a plan that works perfectly for you.

"And I will give them a heart to know Me, for I am the Lord. They will be My people and I will be their God, for they will return to Me with their whole heart."
JEREMIAH 24:7

ACTIVITY:

Ready for a Bible Reading Scavenger Hunt?

You now have all the information you need to start reading and studying God's Word. With your own Bible and the guidelines you've learned, you're ready to dive in. It's time to discover the amazing things God has for you.

So, let's go on an adventure with the Bible Reading Scavenger Hunt! Feel free to ask a friend or family member to do this with you.

Put on your thinking cap, **grab your Bible, and let's get going.** (And yes, of course you can use *any* kind of Bible reading tool to help you with this challenge.)

Hunt 1:

Find a verse that talks about God's love.

Hunt 2:

Find a story in which someone told the truth.

Hunt 3:

Find a verse that includes one of God's promises.

Hunt 4:

Find a story in which someone forgave someone else.

Hunt 5:

Find a verse that talks about God's faithfulness.

Hunt 6:

Find a story about Jesus teaching others.

Hunt 7:

Find a verse that talks about joy.

Hunt 8:

Find a story in which someone trusted God.

Hunt 9:

Find a story in which someone helped a friend.

Hunt 10:

Find a verse that talks about being kind.

Hunt 11:

Find a story in which someone showed courage.

Hunt 12:

Find a verse about being thankful.

Hunt 13:

Find a story in which someone prayed.

Hunt 14:

Find a verse about a shepherd.

Hunt 15:

Find a story in which someone obeyed God.

Have you completed your Bible Reading Scavenger Hunt? How many of those items could you find?

By looking for verses and stories, you're learning how to explore God's Word. And by thinking over what you found, you begin to see how these scriptures apply to your life.

Remember, the Bible is full of wisdom, promises, and lessons that can help you grow closer to God every day. Keep reading! Always ask questions. Search for what God wants to teach you. And never forget that He is always there to help you understand.

You have everything you need to learn your Bible. . .to discover incredible things about God, yourself, and the world around you.

Now, keep going—and enjoy the adventure!

APPENDIX

Here's a Plan to Read Through the Bible in a Year!

DAY 1:
Genesis 1–3

DAY 2:
Genesis 4:1–7:9

DAY 3:
Genesis 7:10–10:32

DAY 4:
Genesis 11–14

DAY 5:
Genesis 15–18

DAY 6:
Genesis 19–21

DAY 7:
Genesis 22–24

DAY 8:
Genesis 25–27

DAY 9:
Genesis 28–29

DAY 10:
Genesis 30–31

DAY 11:
Genesis 32–34

DAY 12:
Genesis 35–36

DAY 13:
Genesis 37–39

DAY 14:
Genesis 40–41

DAY 15:
Genesis 42–43

DAY 16:
Genesis 44–45

DAY 17:
Genesis 46–48

DAY 18:
Genesis 49–50

DAY 19:
Exodus 1–3

DAY 20:
Exodus 4–6

DAY 21:
Exodus 7–9

DAY 22:
Exodus 10–12

DAY 23:
Exodus 13–15

DAY 24:
Exodus 16–18

DAY 25:
Exodus 19–20

DAY 26:
Exodus 21–23

DAY 27:
Exodus 24–27

DAY 28:
Exodus 28–29

DAY 29:
Exodus 30–31

DAY 30:
Exodus 32–33

DAY 31:
Exodus 34–35

DAY 32:
Exodus 36–38

DAY 33:
Exodus 39–40

DAY 34:
Leviticus 1–4

DAY 35:
Leviticus 5–7

DAY 36:
Leviticus 8–10

DAY 37:
Leviticus 11–12

DAY 38:
Leviticus 13:1–14:32

DAY 39:
Leviticus 14:33–15:33

DAY 40:
Leviticus 16–17

DAY 41:
Leviticus 18–20

DAY 42:
Leviticus 21–23

DAY 43:
Leviticus 24–25

DAY 44:
Leviticus 26–27

DAY 45:
Numbers 1–2

DAY 46:
Numbers 3–4

DAY 47:
Numbers 5–6

DAY 48:
Numbers 7

DAY 49:
Numbers 8–10

DAY 50:
Numbers 11–12

DAY 51:
Numbers 13–14

DAY 52:
Numbers 15–16

DAY 53:
Numbers 17–19

DAY 54:
Numbers 20–21

DAY 55:
Numbers 22–24

DAY 56:
Numbers 25–27

DAY 57:
Numbers 28–30

DAY 58:
Numbers 31–32

DAY 59:
Numbers 33–34

DAY 60:
Numbers 35–36

DAY 61:
Deuteronomy 1–2

DAY 62:
Deuteronomy 3–4

DAY 63:
Deuteronomy 5–7

DAY 64:
Deuteronomy 8–11

DAY 65:
Deuteronomy 12–14

DAY 66:
Deuteronomy 15–17

DAY 67:
Deuteronomy 18–20

DAY 68:
Deuteronomy 21–23

DAY 69:
Deuteronomy 24–26

DAY 70:
Deuteronomy 27–28

DAY 71:
Deuteronomy 29–31

DAY 72:
Deuteronomy 32–34

DAY 73:
Joshua 1–2

DAY 74:
Joshua 3–5

DAY 75:
Joshua 6–8

DAY 76:
Joshua 9–10

DAY 77:
Joshua 11–13

DAY 78:
Joshua 14–16

DAY 79:
Joshua 17–19

DAY 80:
Joshua 20–22

DAY 81:
Joshua 23–24

DAY 82:
Judges 1–3

DAY 83:
Judges 4–5

DAY 84:
Judges 6–8

DAY 85:
Judges 9

DAY 86:
Judges 10–12

DAY 87:
Judges 13–16

DAY 88:
Judges 17–19

DAY 89:
Judges 20–21

DAY 90:
Ruth 1–4

DAY 91:
1 Samuel 1–3

DAY 92:
1 Samuel 4–6

DAY 93:
1 Samuel 7–9

DAY 94:
1 Samuel 10–12

DAY 95:
1 Samuel 13–14

DAY 96:
1 Samuel 15–16

DAY 97:
1 Samuel 17–18

DAY 98:
1 Samuel 19–20

DAY 99:
1 Samuel 21–23

DAY 100:
1 Samuel 24–25

DAY 101:
1 Samuel 26–28

DAY 102:
1 Samuel 29–31

DAY 103:
2 Samuel 1–2

DAY 104:
2 Samuel 3–4

DAY 105:
2 Samuel 5–7

DAY 106:
2 Samuel 8–10

DAY 107:
2 Samuel 11–12

DAY 108:
2 Samuel 13–14

DAY 109:
2 Samuel 15–16

DAY 110:
2 Samuel 17–18

DAY 111:
2 Samuel 19–20

DAY 112:
2 Samuel 21–22

DAY 113:
2 Samuel 23–24

DAY 114:
1 Kings 1–2

DAY 115:
1 Kings 3–4

DAY 116:
1 Kings 5–7

DAY 117:
1 Kings 8–9

DAY 118:
1 Kings 10–11

DAY 119:
1 Kings 12–13

DAY 120:
1 Kings 14–15

DAY 121:
1 Kings 16–17

DAY 122:
1 Kings 18–19

DAY 123:
1 Kings 20–21

DAY 124:
1 Kings 22

DAY 125:
2 Kings 1–3

DAY 126:
2 Kings 4–5

DAY 127:
2 Kings 6–8

DAY 128:
2 Kings 9–10

DAY 129:
2 Kings 11–13

DAY 130:
2 Kings 14–15

DAY 131:
2 Kings 16–17

DAY 132:
2 Kings 18–19

DAY 133:
2 Kings 20–21

DAY 134:
2 Kings 22:1–23:30

DAY 135:
2 Kings 23:31–25:30

DAY 136:
1 Chronicles 1–4

DAY 137:
1 Chronicles 5–7

DAY 138:
1 Chronicles 8–10

DAY 139:
1 Chronicles 11–14

DAY 140:
1 Chronicles 15–17

DAY 141:
1 Chronicles 18–21

DAY 142:
1 Chronicles 22–24

DAY 143:
1 Chronicles 25–27

DAY 144:
1 Chronicles 28–29

DAY 145:
2 Chronicles 1–4

DAY 146:
2 Chronicles 5–7

DAY 147:
2 Chronicles 8–9

DAY 148:
2 Chronicles 10–13

DAY 149:
2 Chronicles 14–18

DAY 150:
2 Chronicles 19–21

DAY 151:
2 Chronicles 22–24

DAY 152:
2 Chronicles 25–28

DAY 153:
2 Chronicles 29–30

DAY 154:
2 Chronicles 31–33

DAY 155:
2 Chronicles 34–36

DAY 156:
Ezra 1–3

DAY 157:
Ezra 4–6

DAY 158:
Ezra 7–8

DAY 159:
Ezra 9–10

DAY 160:
Nehemiah 1–3

DAY 161:
Nehemiah 4–6

DAY 162:
Nehemiah 7–9

DAY 163:
Nehemiah 10–11

DAY 164:
Nehemiah 12–13

DAY 165:
Esther 1–3

DAY 166:
Esther 4–6

DAY 167:
Esther 7–10

DAY 168:
Job 1–5

DAY 169:
Job 6–10

DAY 170:
Job 11–14

DAY 171:
Job 15–19

DAY 172:
Job 20–24

DAY 173:
Job 25–31

DAY 174:
Job 32–37

DAY 175:
Job 38–42

DAY 176:
Psalms 1–10

DAY 177:
Psalms 11–18

DAY 178:
Psalms 19–27

DAY 179:
Psalms 28–34

DAY 180:
Psalms 35–39

DAY 181:
Psalms 40–47

DAY 182:
Psalms 48–55

DAY 183:
Psalms 56–65

DAY 184:
Psalms 66–71

DAY 185:
Psalms 72–77

DAY 186:
Psalms 78–82

DAY 187:
Psalms 83–89

DAY 188:
Psalms 90–99

DAY 189:
Psalms 100–105

DAY 190:
Psalms 106–109

DAY 191:
Psalms 110–118

DAY 192:
Psalm 119

DAY 193:
Psalms 120–134

DAY 194:
Psalms 135–142

DAY 195:
Psalms 143–150

DAY 196:
Proverbs 1–5

DAY 197:
Proverbs 6–9

DAY 198:
Proverbs 10–14

DAY 199:
Proverbs 15–19

DAY 200:
Proverbs 20–23

DAY 201:
Proverbs 24–28

DAY 202:
Proverbs 29–31

DAY 203:
Ecclesiastes 1–6

DAY 204:
Ecclesiastes 7–12

DAY 205:
Song 1–8

DAY 206:
Isaiah 1–4

DAY 207:
Isaiah 5–7

DAY 208:
Isaiah 8–10

DAY 209:
Isaiah 11–14

DAY 210:
Isaiah 15–19

DAY 211:
Isaiah 20–23

DAY 212:
Isaiah 24–27

DAY 213:
Isaiah 28–31

DAY 214:
Isaiah 32–35

DAY 215:
Isaiah 36–39

DAY 216:
Isaiah 40–42

DAY 217:
Isaiah 43–45

DAY 218:
Isaiah 46–48

DAY 219:
Isaiah 49–51

DAY 220:
Isaiah 52–56

DAY 221:
Isaiah 57–59

DAY 222:
Isaiah 60–63

DAY 223:
Isaiah 64–66

DAY 224:
Jeremiah 1–3

DAY 225:
Jeremiah 4–6

DAY 226:
Jeremiah 7–9

DAY 227:
Jeremiah 10–12

DAY 228:
Jeremiah 13–15

DAY 229:
Jeremiah 16–19

DAY 230:
Jeremiah 20–22

DAY 231:
Jeremiah 23–25

DAY 232:
Jeremiah 26–28

DAY 233:
Jeremiah 29–30

DAY 234:
Jeremiah 31–32

DAY 235:
Jeremiah 33–35

DAY 236:
Jeremiah 36–38

DAY 237:
Jeremiah 39–41

DAY 238:
Jeremiah 42–44

DAY 239:
Jeremiah 45–47

DAY 240:
Jeremiah 48–49

DAY 241:
Jeremiah 50

DAY 242:
Jeremiah 51–52

DAY 243:
Lamentations 1–2

DAY 244:
Lamentations 3–5

DAY 245:
Ezekiel 1–3

DAY 246:
Ezekiel 4–7

DAY 247:
Ezekiel 8–11

DAY 248:
Ezekiel 12–15

DAY 249:
Ezekiel 16–17

DAY 250:
Ezekiel 18–20

DAY 251:
Ezekiel 21–22

DAY 252:
Ezekiel 23–24

DAY 253:
Ezekiel 25–27

DAY 254:
Ezekiel 28–30

DAY 255:
Ezekiel 31–32

DAY 256:
Ezekiel 33–34

DAY 257:
Ezekiel 35–36

DAY 258:
Ezekiel 37–39

DAY 259:
Ezekiel 40–42

DAY 260:
Ezekiel 43–44

DAY 261:
Ezekiel 45–46

DAY 262:
Ezekiel 47–48

DAY 263:
Daniel 1–2

DAY 264:
Daniel 3–4

DAY 265:
Daniel 5–6

DAY 266:
Daniel 7–9

DAY 267:
Daniel 10–12

DAY 268:
Hosea 1–5

DAY 269:
Hosea 6–10

DAY 270:
Hosea 11–14

DAY 271:
Joel 1–3

DAY 272:
Amos 1–5

DAY 273:
Amos 6–9;
Obadiah

DAY 274:
Jonah 1–4

DAY 275:
Micah 1–7

DAY 276:
Nahum 1–3;
Habakkuk 1–3

DAY 277:
Zephaniah 1–3;
Haggai 1–2

DAY 278:
Zechariah 1–4

DAY 279:
Zechariah 5–9

DAY 280:
Zechariah 10–14

DAY 281:
Malachi 1–4

DAY 282:
Matthew 1–4

DAY 283:
Matthew 5–7

DAY 284:
Matthew 8–9

DAY 285:
Matthew 10–11

DAY 286:
Matthew 12–13

DAY 287:
Matthew 14–16

DAY 288:
Matthew 17–19

DAY 289:
Matthew 20–21

DAY 290:
Matthew 22–23

DAY 291:
Matthew 24–25

DAY 292:
Matthew 26

DAY 293:
Matthew 27–28

DAY 294:
Mark 1–3

DAY 295:
Mark 4–6

DAY 296:
Mark 7–9

DAY 297:
Mark 10–11

DAY 298:
Mark 12–13

DAY 299:
Mark 14–16

DAY 300:
Luke 1

DAY 301:
Luke 2–3

DAY 302:
Luke 4–5

DAY 303:
Luke 6–7

DAY 304:
Luke 8–9

DAY 305:
Luke 10–11

DAY 306:
Luke 12–13

DAY 307:
Luke 14–15

DAY 308:
Luke 16–17

DAY 309:
Luke 18–19

DAY 310:
Luke :
20:1–22:38

DAY 311:
Luke 22:39–24:53

DAY 312:
John 1–3

DAY 313:
John 4–5

DAY 314:
John 6–7

DAY 315:
John 8–9

DAY 316:
John 10–11

DAY 317:
John 12–13

DAY 318:
John 14–16

DAY 319:
John 17–18

DAY 320:
John 19–21

DAY 321:
Acts 1–2

DAY 322:
Acts 3–5

DAY 323:
Acts 6–7

DAY 324:
Acts 8–9

DAY 325:
Acts 10–12

DAY 326:
Acts 13–14

DAY 327:
Acts 15–17

DAY 328:
Acts 18–19

DAY 329:
Acts 20–22

DAY 330:
Acts 23–25

DAY 331:
Acts 26–28

DAY 332:
Romans 1–3

DAY 333:
Romans 4–7

DAY 334:
Romans 8–10

DAY 335:
Romans 11–13

DAY 336:
Romans 14–16

DAY 337:
1 Corinthians 1–6

DAY 338:
1 Corinthians 7–10

DAY 339:
1 Corinthians 11–13

DAY 340:
1 Corinthians 14–16

DAY 341:
2 Corinthians 1–5

DAY 342:
2 Corinthians 6–9

DAY 343:
2 Corinthians 10–13

DAY 344:
Galatians 1–6

DAY 345:
Ephesians 1–6

DAY 346:
Philippians 1–4

DAY 347:
Colossians 1–4

DAY 348:
1 Thessalonians 1–5; 2 Thessalonians 1–3

DAY 349:
1 Timothy 1–6

DAY 350:
2 Timothy 1–4; Titus 1–3

DAY 351:
Philemon; Hebrews 1–6

DAY 352:
Hebrews 7–10

DAY 353:
Hebrews 11–13

DAY 354:
James 1–5

DAY 355:
1 Peter 1–5

DAY 356:
2 Peter 1–3

DAY 357:
1 John 1–5

DAY 358:
2 John; 3 John; Jude

DAY 359:
Revelation 1–3

DAY 360:
Revelation 4–6

DAY 361:
Revelation 7–10

DAY 362:
Revelation 11–13

DAY 363:
Revelation 14–16

DAY 364:
Revelation 17–19

DAY 365:
Revelation 20–22